TI

EXPERIENCE GUERNSEY

HANDBOOK©

2018 Edition

by

Tony Brassell

East Coast Sunrise, Guernsey, December 2017

Cover Image, Guernsey Sunrise

Dedicated to my wonderful family.

Photos by Tony Brassell unless otherwise credited.

ISBN-13: 978-1982047634
ISBN-10: 1982047631

Introduction

In 2017, St Peter Port in Guernsey was given the accolade of being named in the top five best cruise destinations in Britain and Western Europe and in 2017, Aurigny, our local airline, won the best short haul airline category in a Which? Consumer Survey, so maybe it isn't only me that believes Guernsey is one of the best places in the world to live and a pretty awesome place to visit.

Why do I say that?

Well I have lived here all my life and like all residents of similar places we can easily take our homes for granted, but some days, when the sun is shining, the sea is flat calm, a cruise ship sits between the Islands and everyone around you is smiling and says hi, you remember just how really amazing this place is and how it might look to people who have never been here before.

One of my twin daughters spends her summers working for Island Rib Voyages, a local boat cruise business, providing sight-seeing tours around the Islands coast. From time to time we get the opportunity to go out on one of their rib tours and they are brilliant fun, the experience never dulls.

I have seen places I had never seen before, looked at Atlantic Grey seals and puffins and on one memorable occasion saw a pod of dolphins, which was amazing. My son works for Sark Shipping occasionally and he too has seen dolphins on his trips to Sark.

His links with Sark gave me the opportunity to have a trip there recently and again it was a fantastic experience. My wife and I enjoyed a carriage ride, a great stay at Stocks Hotel and several walks around the quiet Sark "roads".

Memorable days which will remain with us for the rest of our lives.

With friends in Alderney, and our favourite Channel Island hotel being located in that Island, we need little excuse to go there too and of course Jersey is just a ten-minute flight away and well worth a visit if you have time during your stay in Guernsey.

If fact all the Islands are beautiful, and the environment changes with the seasons, the weather and the direction of the wind, so no two days are ever the same. We have cliffs, beaches, walks and history in abundance. All within a few square miles.

You can work out, wear yourself out or relax in resplendent peace and quiet – the choice is yours. Guernsey and its Bailiwick can be what you want it to be. You just need to know what you want and where to look for it. Hopefully this Handbook will save you some time with your search and you will experience your perfect holiday.

Guernsey is one of several Islands in the Bay of St Malo, easily accessible by air from many UK and European locations, including Gatwick and Southampton and by sea from South Coast ports and St Malo in France.

Once a popular location for a 2-week beach holiday, it has become increasingly popular as a short break destination for independent travelers, as well as being a regular stop for Cruise liners.

The Bailiwick of Guernsey is a group of Islands (under the control of a Bailiff), which includes Alderney, Sark and Herm. All are within sight of each other which gives the location an almost tropical quality with views across to the other Islands from all but the West Coast of Guernsey, which faces the Atlantic.

On a bright summers day, the views from St Peter Port in Guernsey are some of the finest in the world.

St Peter Port has become a cosmopolitan town, full of fine restaurants and niche retail outlets, while remaining steeped in history and folklore.

In Guernsey, there is something for everyone. If you like walking along cliff paths or jumping into the sea from the bottom of the cliffs, we do that.

If you like small boats, fishing or lazing on beaches, we can do that too. If cycling is for you or just exploring country lanes in the car – well you know what I am going to say.

I have lived here for more than 60 years and still find new corners, new views and new things to do all the time, so your break in Guernsey can easily be filled with activities, if you want it to be.

However, if relaxing is your idea of heaven, Guernsey is one of the best places in the world to do that. The pace of life outside of St Peter Port is relaxed to say the least, with great hotels and restaurants ideally placed to make your visit truly wonderful. Get out the paints, stroll the cliffs, take stunning photographs, lie on a beach, take a boat trip to another island and live your dreams.

One thing I can guarantee is you will never forget your visit to Guernsey and like many people before you, you might just keep coming back for more.

In the following pages I will set out all the information you will need to enjoy a wonderful holiday in the beautiful, British, Channel Island of Guernsey.

You may even want to move here.

If you do, visit – www.locateguernsey.com

The sections covered in this book include:

- About the Handbook
- An Introduction to Guernsey
- Travelling to Guernsey
- Where to Stay
- What to See and Do in Guernsey
- Experience Guernsey Month by Month
- Eating Out
- Shopping
- Getting Around
- The other Islands around Guernsey
- Useful Information
- About the Author

This is the fourth edition of this Handbook which evolved out of the successful Guide to Guernsey which I guess makes this our seventh edition.

This Handbook is constantly evolving in the light of comments and advice we have received and this year we have added some extra images for you to enjoy.

We hope you will really like reading all about our Island and if you choose to visit, have a wonderful time while you are here.

About this Handbook

The Experience Guernsey handbook has been developed from my earlier Handbooks and is designed to provide information about the Island which the visitor can use as a reference. In a new section we will set out what happens in Guernsey during the year as experienced by the locals.

I have inserted more web links so those with access to wifi or who have the 3G and 4G enabled Kindles can use the browser to link to the various websites we list.

As the Kindle Fire and later models are now widespread I shall also include more photographs of the Island so that you can get a better idea of what Guernsey is like.

All visitors to Guernsey should visit the Guernsey Information Centre, as soon as they can, to see what is happening during their stay. They also have a great range of local books and souvenirs if you want to take presents home for the family. Most Hotels and Guest Houses will also have racks of brochures giving you a good idea of what there is to do.

As soon as you arrive, whether it be at the Airport or Harbour you should be able to pick up a free map of the Island which will help you find your way around.

If you do intend driving, please take note of the section in this Guide on driving in Guernsey as there are many different rules which you need to be aware of as soon as you drive away from the Harbour or Airport. The Filter in Turn junctions you most certainly need to be aware of as they can cause accidents for those who don't know how they work.

Please remember that the maximum speed limit in the island is 35 mph. Around the towns it is 25mph and in some areas around schools it can be 20mph.

When you are at the Guernsey Information Centre pick up a parking clock as many parking areas, especially in St Peter Port, have timed parking and you will need to set your clock when you park. Parking is free but the clock costs a couple of pounds.

Within the Handbook we'll offer you some ideas as to what to do on a day out but there are loads of things to do in Guernsey so please, as suggested, visit the Guernsey Information Centre and see what is on offer during your stay. Also look for the events diary which will give you some idea of the festivals and events that are going on while you are in the Island

In the past we have tried to include as many dates of events as possible, however this year we have included the monthly diary as dates often change and new events are added, so we recommend you look at the printed events diary while you are here and check out the www.visitguernsey.com website before you book your journey.

We have established an Experience Guernsey Facebook page which we will populate as the year passes to give the reader a first-hand look at the Island as the year goes by.

The printed event diary can be found at all hotels, guest houses and self-catering accommodation.

Above all this Handbook is designed to try and help you enjoy your visit to Guernsey.

An Introduction to the Location, History and Culture of Guernsey

Located in the Bay of St Malo, on the edge of the English Channel, Guernsey is less than a hundred miles south of the English south coast and thirty or so miles from the French Coast. It is around 24 square miles in area, with one airport and a main harbour, which caters for passenger and freight traffic. It also has a smaller harbour which is used for materials such as coal and fuel.

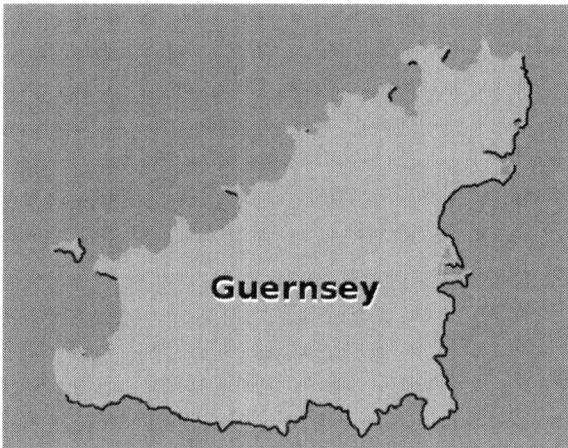

Guernsey is part of a Bailiwick, a group of Islands under the control of a Bailiff. The Bailiff is the head of the legal system. The other Islands in the group include Alderney, Sark, Herm, Breqhou and Jethou. Guernsey is a short, 10-minute flight from Jersey, the largest of the Channel Islands, and a separate jurisdiction.

The History of Guernsey is as long as it is unique and fascinating. Guernsey became an Island about 10,000 years ago when the land bridge to France succumbed to rising sea levels. Evidence of Neolithic man has been found dating back over 8,000 years and the many burial mounds, dolmens and menhirs on the Island are some of the oldest in Europe.

There are three Dolmens on the Island that you can walk into, the best being the Dehus Dolmen at Bordeaux in the North of the Island. Iron Age man settled on the Island and the Romans also used Guernsey as a useful staging post when crossing the Channel.

Ownership of property on the Island helps us understand some of its history, with records dating back to before 1066.

The lands of Normandy in France were at one time under the control of the Bretons. These lands were taken over by Vikings, under the leadership of Rollo.

Their conquests led to the creation of the Duchy of Normandy which included the Channel Islands.

It is conceivable that when William the Conqueror, the Duke of Normandy, invaded England and fought Harold at the Battle of Hastings in 1066, that people from the Islands were part of his army. Certainly, after the battle, Guernsey landowners also became owners of land in England and that impacted on the future nationality of the Islands and the prosperity the Islands enjoy today.

As part of the Duchy of Normandy, the Islands existed in relative peace and tranquility for many years, but in time France was reunited and in the agreement made by King John and Phillippe Augustus of France in 1204, the Islands were forgotten.

The story is told that the wealthy landowners were asked to decide if the Islands wanted to remain as part of Great Britain or France. It seems the landowners must have had more interests in England as they chose to be part of Great Britain

The Islands have remained British ever since, despite rare attempts by the French to seize them back. The arrangement was officially recognised in 1254, when the Islands were annexed to the Crown of England.

As a reward for their loyalty to the British Crown, the Islands were given the right to make their own laws. That moment in history has allowed the Islands to retain their status as Crown Dependencies, answerable to the British Monarchy rather than the British Government.

With the ongoing threat of French attacks, many fortifications were built to protect the Island. The most spectacular of these is Castle Cornet which guards the harbour of St Peter Port. Work on that Castle began around 1204 and for most of its history it remained a short boat ride away from the Island.

Castle Cornet, St Peter Port.

The Castle's most active period was probably during the English Civil War when it remained loyal to the Crown while the Island sided with Cromwell. Periodic shelling took place but the story goes that as the Commander of the garrison in the Castle owned property in St Peter Port, targets were selected very carefully!

The Castle remained loyal to the Crown throughout the Civil War, being supplied by sea from Jersey. As a mark of that loyalty, and I believe by Royal command, the Union Jack, as opposed to the Guernsey flag, is always flown from the flagstaff at the top of the Castle.

The next period of intense defence building came when Napoleon began his reign in France and conquered large swathes of Europe. The Islanders firmly believed they could be invaded at any time and as such the garrison on the Island was strengthened, as were the defences.

At that time, the Island was actually two Islands with the Northern part separated from the main Island by the Braye. There was a Bridge at St Sampsons Harbour and that shopping area is still known locally as "The Bridge".

To ensure that troops could be moved quickly to the Northern defences in the event of an attack, the Braye was filled in and the Military Road created. That road is still, I believe, the longest and straightest road on the Island.

Other larger roads were created to move troops to the West Coast and these "major" roads remain the Island's main thoroughfares to this day.

In the event, all of this activity proved a suitable deterrent and Guernsey never came under attack. An interesting side story is that thousands of Russian troops were rested on the Island during the Napoleonic War.

They were billeted on what is now Delancey Park near my home – it seems amazing to think that 200 years ago thousands of Russian troops were living on that park within a few yards of where I live, maybe even on the land where my house was built.

A few of them died while they were here and a small graveyard near the Vale Castle marks the spot where they were buried.

As a location, the Islands didn't feature in the First World War but at the time Guernsey had its own Militia which fought bravely on the Western front. Members of The Militia or Royal Guernsey Light Infantry as it was called in the war, died in large numbers in the trenches at Passchendaele, Cambrai and then at the Battle of Lys.

After they returned from the First World War what was left of the militia was disbanded. Efforts were made to restart it and a small force was created between the wars but this was disbanded in 1940 for the duration of the war. Many of those men went on to fight in the British armed forces but the Militia would not reform again after the war.

Much of the history of the militia and the defence of Guernsey is portrayed in Castle Cornet and the many excellent museums around the Island.

Fort Grey, off Guernsey's West Coast

The Island's strategic position between England and France, and its strong trading and nautical history, has made the Island an important location and worth defending.

When travelling around Guernsey you can't miss the various forts and Castles which date back over 800 years.

Arguably, however, even more striking are the German defences left after the Occupation of the Islands during the Second World War. The Channel Islands were the only British territories in the European theatre of operations to be occupied by the Germans during the Second World War. The Occupation lasted for 5 years and the occupiers invested heavily in defending the Islands to ensure they would not be recaptured.

Large numbers of German troops were garrisoned on the Islands and Alderney was used as a concentration camp. Over 100 German soldiers died on the Island over the 5 years and a Military Cemetery at Fort George became their final resting place.

Since the Second World War the Island has enjoyed a period of stability and growth. After the war, the tomato growing industry flourished, but this declined in the eighties and Finance took over as the dominant sector supported by a strong manufacturing sector.

In recent years Finance has continued to grow and is now supported by a mix of tourism, creative, manufacturing, IT and a myriad of smaller industries.

The Government of Guernsey is carried out by the States of Deliberation which consists of 38 members from Guernsey, elected by the local residents. There are no party politics and each member stands for election by their own manifesto. You can see how the States of Guernsey is made up on this website - www.gov.gg/deputies

The Island is split into ten parishes and each has a certain amount of control over such things as refuse collection, street lighting and the like. Most States Deputies are elected by members of the public from their parish but some of the more sparsely populated west coast parishes are amalgamated together for election purposes while the more populated St Peter Port is split into two.

The States of Guernsey is divided into Departments, each responsible for different aspects of the Islands management, such as Education, Health and the Environment. Each Department is headed up by a President.

Full details of how the States is run can be found on the www.gov.gg website.

With such strong links to France the Island has retained its own patois language, closely linked to Norman French. Usage is limited these days though attempts to revive it through the Islands school children are being made. Guernsey Laws also have their origin in Norman Law and local Advocates (lawyers) have to study in France for a period of time. Road names and house names are still mostly in French.

Over the last 50 years the Islands have developed in many ways. The demise of the tomato industry has left many derelict greenhouses on the Island while the growth of the Finance Industry has seen the construction of many new office buildings in and around the Island's capital, St Peter Port.

However, the local planners have confined most new development to the areas around St Peter Port, St Sampson's and the North of Guernsey, leaving the south of the Island, and the southern cliffs almost unchanged over the last few decades.

The people of Guernsey are by and large friendly and hospitable. Around 63,000 people live in the Island and the majority are local. They are hard working and often have more than one job.

Fishing, horticulture, retailing and traditional trades are still strong on the Island. If you are lost and need help, just ask. You will be surprised just how helpful some people can be.

A small Guernsey Fishing Boat.

It isn't unknown for people to give lifts or to say follow me to show visitors the way they want to go.

To be honest the Island is also so small, once you find your way to the coast, you will find it quite easy to get around.

The Bus service is great too and you may be lucky to enjoy a ride on one of their new buses which include stop by stop information, so you will know where to get off. If you are unsure just ask the driver for help. There aren't many places that you can't get to easily, either by bus or on foot.

How to Get to Guernsey

As an Island, Guernsey has developed a range of air and sea links offering the visitor several options. By sea there are fast ferry services from Poole on the south coast of England, with a slower, all weather ferry operating from Portsmouth.

A new high-speed catamaran is on the Channel Islands route which should improve the service even further.

Condor Liberation

There are also sea links to the French Coast, again by fast ferry to St Malo and a relatively new but less frequent service to the Normandy coast at Dielette. Travel to the Islands of Jersey, Alderney, Sark and Herm is also possible by sea and air. A new Uber style aircraft service called Waves is being trialed and it will be interesting to see if this comes into full operation during 2018.

By air you can travel from a number of UK Airports, directly to Guernsey. These include Gatwick, Southampton, Manchester, Birmingham and Stansted. Direct links also operate into Dinan near St Malo, Jersey and Alderney.

With a single flight change you can access the Island from almost anywhere.

New routes are under consideration all the time and it is worth looking at the various websites run by the airlines to see what the current links are. Operators include:

By Sea:-
Condor Ferries
www.condorferries.co.uk
01202 207216 (UK)

Condor Ferry leaving St Peter Port.

By Air:-

Flybe
www.flybe.co.uk
0871 700 2000 (UK)

Flybe Aircraft Leaving Guernsey Airport

Aurigny

www.aurigny.com

01481 822886

The New Member of the Aurigny Fleet – Embraer ERJ 190

Blue Islands

www.blueislands.com
Tel: 08456 202122

Blue Islands Aircraft at Guernsey Airport

Travel to the Island can be expensive, particularly if you wait until the last minute to book. Cheap seats are normally available for bookings made well in advance, making the Islands far more affordable than commonly thought.

When booking air travel on line be sure to check out the full price, including airport taxes, baggage and allocated seating as this can increase the cost of the flights considerably. When travelling by sea, the ferries from the UK can accommodate vehicles. Bringing your car to Guernsey can be an attractive option but if your stay is short it may be cheaper to hire a car when on the Island.

Hire car companies include:

Avis - 08706060100 (National Call)
Europcar - 01481 237638
Hertz - 0800 7351014
Harlequin Hire Cars - 01481 239511
Falles Hire Cars - 01481 236902

We will discuss getting around on Guernsey later in the book as there are some very different driving rules on the Island roads which you need to know about before getting into your car.

You can also bring motorbikes and cycles to Guernsey on the ferry but again both can be hired on the Island.

Guernsey Airport

Where to Stay?

There is a wide range of Hotels, Guest Houses and Self-Catering accommodation on Guernsey. Prices are available to suit every pocket and a comprehensive list of accommodation is available on the Visit Guernsey web site at www.visitguernsey.com

However, we have several that we think are worth consideration, not because we have any interest in them but because we like the location and the facilities they have to offer.

On the West Coast of the Island is the Cobo Bay Hotel. If you choose this hotel, try and get a room with a balcony overlooking Cobo Bay. It may cost extra but if you are lucky enough to enjoy one or two of the spectacular Guernsey sunsets while you are there, it will be worth it.

One of the more exclusive hotels is La Grande Mare Hotel, also on the Island's West Coast, this time at Vazon Bay. It has its own 18-hole Golf Course, outdoor and indoor swimming pools with a gym and health club. There is also a tennis court, putting green and driving range, linked to an American Golf shop for all your golf equipment.

We have stayed at the Grande Mare a few times and the service and quality are always excellent. They do an amazing afternoon, champagne tea and often have offers on for overnight stays with a meal and breakfast.

The best hotel for the south coast bays and cliffs in our view is the Bella Luce.

If you want to spend your time in the Island's capital, St Peter Port, the Old Government House Hotel (OGH) and Moore's Hotel would be good choices. The OGH is the better of the two in terms of facilities with an excellent Health Club and restaurant. They also set up an Alpine Lodge in December and have promised me they will be setting it up again in 2018.

All the Hotels we mention have excellent restaurants and are renowned for their good service.

Slightly further out of town are the Duke of Richmond Hotel which is close to the Island's main Leisure Centre and Cambridge Park, La Fregate Hotel, which is renowned for its first-class service and the Hotel de Havelet which has wonderful views over St Peter Port Harbour and Castle Cornet.

Out of town you have a choice of beautiful country hotels, each with their own attributes. Some of our favourites include the St Pierre Park Hotel which has a nine-hole par 3 golf course with a modern range and brand new pirate themed crazy golf course, La Trelade, La Villette, the Hougue Du Pommier, La Barbarie, the Jerbourg Hotel (on the cliffs), Les Douvres and the Farmhouse.

One of newest hotels, specifically designed for the over 50's, but not exclusively so, is the Fermain Valley Hotel. The food there is exceptional, and they have one of the finest restaurants on Guernsey attached to the Hotel.

We stayed at the Fermain Valley just before Christmas at the end of 2014 and a few times since and I can say with confidence that the rooms are beautifully designed and the facilities were brilliant.

Despite it being December, we enjoyed a cliff walk and then a swim in the heated indoor pool and later a wonderful meal in their nautical themed restaurant.

The next morning, we sat on our balcony and watched the sun rise over Jersey – see image.

Breakfast was amazing and the staff couldn't have been more helpful. A very special hotel.

We also had the opportunity to stay at the Farmhouse Hotel in December 2014. It is located near the Airport. The rooms were very well appointed and the meals were wonderful. You don't have sea views from this hotel and the pool wasn't open at that time of year, but I would say the food was as good, if not better than the Fermain Valley, especially the choice for breakfast.

If you are wondering how as a local we can use these hotels and stay over, particularly in the winter months, it is because there are some local deals websites where you can sample these wonderful hotels and restaurants at bargain prices. I subscribe to a website called www.quidsin.com. This is worth considering as while you are visiting you might get the chance to take advantage of one of these offers and enjoy a nice meal out for half the normal price.

A full list of these and other hotels, together with their phone numbers is set out in the appendices.

Guest Houses on Guernsey are reducing in number but a few good ones are still available and a list of our favourites is in the appendices.

Self-Catering Bungalows are a popular choice on Guernsey and though they too have reduced in number there are new ones available and more are being built.

Vazon Bay Holiday Apartments

The Vazon Bay Apartments are a popular choice and the 4-star Wisteria Apartments attached to the Fleur du Jardin Hotel look excellent. They are both nicely located being just a short walk from the West Coast beaches.

The Vazon Bay Apartments are more suited to families and are actually within yards of the Island's West Coast. They have their own pool and are next to a very popular restaurant. The same applies to those at the Collinette Hotel.

A full list of self-catering apartments is available on the Visit Guernsey web site but listed in the appendices are the contact details for some of those that we would suggest, simply by location and reputation.

L'Aumone House Barn

Camping

The three main campsites on Guernsey are listed below, for those who like living under canvas.

If you want to bring your mobile home to Guernsey, you need to check with the campsite first as I believe only a limited number of pitches are available.

Please check availability with the sites before making any firm travel arrangements.

The sites are:

Fauxquets Valley Farm	01481 255460
La Bailloterie, Vale	01481 243636
Vaugrat Camping	01481 257468

Keeping in Touch

Most of the bigger hotels will offer you free wifi during your stay but if you like to catch up with the news and access the internet while drinking a cup of tea or coffee there are a couple of places we would recommend.

Along "the front" near the roundabout with the ships mast you will find the Urban Kitchen which offers meals as well as teas and coffees. They offer free wifi as does Muse, another 100 yards or so North of the same roundabout.

If you like french surroundings, the Petit Café, next to the taxi rank alongside the same roundabout also offers free wifi and excellent tea and coffee plus a full menu.

So now you have no excuse for not checking Facebook and telling the world what a fabulous holiday you are having!

If you are visiting and plan to do some work while you are here and need a base for a few hours a day or week then look no further than the Digital Greenhouse. This is a space designed especially to develop Digital Businesses in the Island and places are available to rent for short periods. If you need somewhere to plug in your computer, enjoy great wifi and continue with your blog or whatever you are working on, in a fun business environment, check out the Digital Greenhouse.

To find out more about this excellent facility, visit www.digitalgreenhouse.gg

What to See and Do in Guernsey?

There are many things to see and do in Guernsey for people of all ages and whatever their interests. If you would like to explore the scenic aspect of the Island, you can walk the cliffs, wander through the lanes and visit the beaches.

Some places are a must see, like Castle Cornet, Fort Grey, Victor Hugo's House, the Little Chapel and the Occupation Museums. Hidden prehistoric Dolmens, secluded bays and sites of special ecological significance can be harder to find.

At certain times of the year there are areas worthy of a visit. At the end of April and early May the Bluebell Woods on the Island's East coast can be spectacular. The cliffs in spring are also amazing with a riot of colour with flowers and gorse in full bloom.

If you want to see Puffins, they only visit Herm during the spring and if you are on the sea in the summer you may be lucky enough to see dolphins around our East Coast.

Tours of the Island can be arranged by taxi or though the tour operators. They will take you to see many of the interesting places and some of the tours are specific such as Occupation tours and I believe they do a Guernsey Literary and Potato Peel Pie Society tour now.

They will also take you to the usual Tourist attractions such as Guernsey Pearl, Oatlands and Guernsey Candles.

While these can be worth a visit if you are hunting for souvenirs, they are also easily found and are not the hidden treasures that the taxi firms can show you and which many visitors never see.

If you are interested in prehistoric history, it is worth seeking out the Dehus Dolmen at Bordeaux. There you can enter the grave chamber and by using the lighting put in place just for the purpose, highlight the carving in one of the large stones which form the roof.

Just watch your head as you enter the chamber, it is very low.

Entrance to Le Creux es Faies
Dolmen at L'Eree

When you visit Guernsey, there are often events on you should look out for. The Guernsey Event Diary will give you details of such events as will the events list on the website at www.visitguernsey.com.

You can also get an up to date view on what is happening during your stay by visiting the Guernsey Information Centre on the seafront in the heart of St Peter Port.

Look out for special exhibitions at the Guernsey Museum in Candie Gardens.

On May the 9th the Island celebrates the anniversary of Liberation from the German Occupation at the end of the Second World War, and there are events each year to mark the occasion, which if you are in the Island at that time, you can enjoy.

To highlight what goes on we will take you through the Guernsey Experience on a month by month basis, explaining what is happening and giving you our experiences of the various events we have enjoyed over the past few years.

Experience Guernsey Month by Month

January

January is usually a quiet month, common with many other places in the world. After the celebrations of Christmas and the New Year people tend to hunker down until the next pay day and let the bad weather pass them by until at least one or two pay packets have restored their bank accounts enough for them to start going out and enjoying themselves again.

That is unless the January sales in St Peter Port tempt you to part with more hard-earned cash in search of a bargain.

However, this year, as I write this chapter, January has seen some amazingly pleasant weather and not everything to do on Guernsey costs money. While some restaurants close for a few weeks, people are out walking the beaches and the cliffs, strolling around the lanes and the parks and generally burning off a few of those extra calories that were put on during the festivities.

Many great offers are available at those hotels and restaurants that remain open and if you do choose to visit in January, and February for that matter, you can have a wonderful time.

You won't be sunning yourselves and getting a tan, as the temperatures drop substantially when the skies are clear, but if you are a fan of those lovely, peaceful days, when the air is crisp and you can see for miles then Guernsey can be the place for you.

My diary from the last few years is full of long walks, often followed by lovely meals out in front of warm fires, in short just enjoying the good days that January and February can bring.

Obviously, it isn't always like that and there are times when it rains and blows a gale. But watching the sea throw itself against the sea walls on the west coast has a beauty all of its own.

Sun rises and sunsets seem particularly spectacular at this time of year and I have included some on our Experience Guernsey Facebook page for your enjoyment.

There are numerous theatrical events and shows during the winter months including a pantomime or two. Oddsocks performed in the Island in January 2017 with their adaptation of Jungle Book and my daughter thoroughly enjoyed it. The museums are open with many displays and the farmers markets are in full swing on Saturdays near the end of the month and then throughout the year.

Also during January there are many sporting fixtures to enjoy with in particular, Guernsey FC playing their home games at Footes Lane and the Guernsey Rugby Club, also playing at the same venue in their home games within the UK national leagues.

This year we bought ourselves an overnight stay at La Grande Mare Hotel which included an evening meal, breakfast and afternoon champagne tea. This was though Quidsin.com and was excellent value. We were given a penthouse which included a living area with kitchen, a huge bathroom and a large bedroom.

The meal was fantastic, and breakfast was brilliant. Champagne afternoon tea was also excellent, and the staff were wonderful throughout our stay. My wife and I would highly recommend this hotel. We didn't use the gym or pool during our short stay, but these facilities are excellent too.

February

The Island will still be gripped by the chills of winter during February but again there will be good days and already it will feel noticeably warmer as the month goes on.

Those Islanders who still run greenhouses will be planting away and the sports events will be in full swing throughout the month as the winter seasons near the end.

In the diary for February 2017, the first of the Guided Walks takes place at Cobo on the 18th of the month. Entitled "Casemates, Canals and Curios" it started in the Grandes Roques Car Park starting at 1.30 pm. It took over 2 and a half hours and cost £8. The Guide was Andy Walker.

Having taken a local walking tour myself I can highly recommend these events which are thoroughly interesting and good exercise. A drink or a warming meal at the Rockmount, next to the Cobo Bay Hotel, after such a walk is highly recommended.

The Farmers markets continue though the month and of course the Museums and Art Galleries are open. During February in 2016 we visited the Candie Museum and saw a great Lego models and art exhibition.

In 2016, we visited the beautiful Fermain Valley Hotel for Valentine's Day and my Facebook page is full of pictures from the restaurant and of views from our room overlooking Fermain Bay to the East.

There are also a number of lovely photos of sunrises and high tides on our Facebook page in February, another trademark of this time of year. By the end of the month thoughts move to spring, daffodils are in full bloom and the gardens are starting to come to life. The sun starts to feel warm on the skin and the sun beds are put out in the garden.

It is also worth checking what's on at Beau Sejour while you visit. There are a number of events there throughout the year and if course they have the Island's largest cinema.

Their website is www.beausejour.gg

March

The events start to build as the year warms up and at the end of March the Guernsey Arts Commission organize a Lantern Parade through St Peter Port. The Arts Commission have an active diary of events which you can find on www.arts.gg.

The Farmers Markets continue through the month and in 2017 there was another Guided Walk, this time around Saumarez Park, the Island's premier park on the 18th of the month.

At the Candie Museum there was an Exhibition of photographs from the Wildlife Photographer of the Year and halfway through the month they changed to an exhibition of portraits from their collection. Full details of their diary can be found on www.museums.gov.gg

By the end of the month Island Rib Voyages will be in full swing. We enjoyed a great trip out with them at the end of March in 2016. The sea was flat calm, and the sky was sunny and clear. There were plenty more trips with them during the course of that year and through 2017.

Already in 2017 dolphins have been seen off the Island's East Coast and they were regular visitors in 2017.

On the 31st March the noon day gun will start firing again for the summer from Castle Cornet. Always worth a visit, Castle Cornet is open in the first quarter of the year from 10am to 3pm. During the summer the hours are extended to 10am to 5pm. There are also a number of events held there throughout the year including outdoor concerts and re-enactments. Castle Cornet has been part of the St Peter Port view for 800 years and was designed to protect the approach to St Peter Port Harbour.

April

As soon as we reach April the season really kicks off and visitor numbers start to swell. There can be amazingly good weather at this time of year, although the evenings can still be cold. You will see people sitting outside enjoying Al Fresco dining around St Peter Port and outside some of the coastal hotels and restaurants.

With the days drawing out locals can enjoy their recreational time after work as well as at the weekends and the beaches and cliffs start to get busy.

There are loads of Guided tours to choose from and boating becomes real fun with regular trips on Island Ribs available. Trips to Herm and Sark become more regular.

If Easter is in April this is usually the time that many attractions re-open their doors as visitor numbers swell. The marinas usually start to get busy and the first cruise ships start to appear. The Petit Train starts its tours around St Peter Port at Easter and the ringing of its bell marks the sound of spring in St Peter Port.

Victor, the Petit Train

On the 8th of April in 2017 the Guernsey Heritage Festival began and ran for the rest of the month and then into May. Hundreds of events were held across the Islands and the full programme can be seen on this link –

http://www.visitguernsey.com/sites/visitguernsey/files/2017_ci_heritage_festival_guide.pdf

The Heritage festival covered the whole history of the Islands up until modern times. Anyone interested in Heritage would have a field day with so many fascinating well-organized events taking place.

It's also a good time to think about a visit to Herm. As the days get warmer the beauty of spring in Herm is not to be underestimated.

The Trident leaving for Herm from St Peter Port

May

As we move into May the popular Seafront Sundays begin.

These are themed events held on the Crown pier and along the sea front from the main roundabout as far as the Town Church. Each event includes local crafts and food products as well as the object of the event. These can be local food, motor sport, pets, sport and the like. They are held throughout the summer, the last usually taking place around the end of August or early September.

If you get a chance, make sure you visit the Bluebell woods at the start of May or the end of April to see this spectacular annual event.

At the start of the month, during the first Bank Holiday weekend there is usually a Horse Racing event at L'Ancresse Common. Sadly in 2017 that weekend coincided with the only bad weather we had experienced in weeks and the event had to be cancelled but I am sure it will be back again for 2018.

May also includes the Islands Liberation Day which is a Bank Holiday in Guernsey. This marks the day the German Occupying forces surrendered to the British Military ending 5 long years of occupation. Most years there is a cavalcade to mark the event as well as numerous other functions. The whole day culminates with a firework display in St Peter Port.

See a video of the cavalcade on the Visit Guernsey Facebook page on-

https://www.facebook.com/VisitGuernsey/videos/101543655 71162312/

In Alderney, they don't celebrate Liberation Day as Guernsey people do as the Alderney residents didn't return to that Island until December 1945. So, they hold a celebration in December each year to mark Homecoming Day.

Many major sporting events are held in May each year, including the Muratti, which is usually the climax of the Channel Island football calendar. The match is usually between Guernsey and Jersey, but there is a semi-final when Alderney take on one of the two main Islands. They haven't played in a final since 1938 when the system was different. Alderney haven't won the trophy since 1920.

The Guernsey Heritage Festival was quickly followed by the Guernsey Literary Festival which took place between the 10th and 14th May. This is a great event for anyone interested in being a writer or who just wants to hear writers talk about their work and their lives. A packed programme was held in 2017 and I am sure there will be more in 2018.

You can find out what is happening on their website at:-
http://www.guernseyliteraryfestival.com/

Continuing with the Festival theme, the Spring Walking Festival started on the 20th May in 2017 and carried on into June. It gives everyone the chance to walk and learn about the history, flora and fauna of the island while enjoying some of our spectacular scenery. There are usually walks in Herm too for those wishing to see more of that Island.

With three Bank Holidays in May the Islanders usually take full advantage with events like the Balcony Gigs at the Cobo Bay Hotel, Hill Climb motor racing on the Val des Terres and of course all the events surrounding Liberation Day.

June

Now the weather really hots up and events crop up thick and fast. The walking festival continued in 2017 and concerts were held in Candie Gardens.

Island Rib Voyages can take you to see our Atlantic Grey Seal colony – see below - and the temporary resident puffins in Puffin Bay at the back of Herm Island.

Sand Racing takes place on the Island beaches and in June 2017 the International Sand Ace British Championships were held at Vazon Bay on the 24th.

One of the most popular Sea Front Sundays was held on the 11th June 2017 with Taste Guernsey taking over the sea front. The sun shone, and stalls and Al Fresco dining filled the streets for this popular event.

There was a Cider and Ale Festival in Herm the following week and the week after the newly refurbished Guernsey Aquarium opened its doors for the first time in 2017.

Alderney held its own Food Festival near the end of June and people started travelling to Sark for their famous Folk Festival which started on the 1st July.

An Atlantic Grey Seal off the Island of Herm

July

As well as the music in Sark, Castle Cornet is alive with music as the ever-popular KPMG Castle Nights started on the 15th July 2017. Held for 4 consecutive Fridays, these free to attend events are loved by locals and visitors alike, with many people taking picnics and spending the evenings sitting on blankets in the Castle grounds listening to a diverse range of music in these historic surroundings. Doors open at 6pm and the events go on until about 9pm.

Guernsey's traditional show, the Viaer Marchi starts the show season off on the evening of the first Monday in July. There you will see traditional crafts, Guernsey Dancing, historical displays as well as loads of food and drink stands and other stalls with a local flavor. It is well known that the sun always shines on the Viaer Marchi (well almost always) and this traditional event attracts people in their thousands. It is held in Saumarez Park, starting at 5pm.

Guernsey people are also big supporters of local charities and in July 2017 there was an event called 30 Bays in 30 Days where people set out to swim in thirty different bays during the month in support of Les Bourgs Hospice. This is Epic also organized a major event this month with the organisers trying to encourage Islanders to do something Epic during the week like 7 marathons in 7 days.

As a visitor I am not suggesting you participate in such events but if you are wondering what is happening on certain days when you see people running or walking along the coast in wild get ups it won't come as such a shock! It's all for charity.

Seafront Sundays are a regular event in July and August so look out for those and the balcony gigs and other concerts are a frequent occurrence. We enjoyed a picnic in Candie Gardens listening to a Beatles tribute band called the Day Trippers in 2017. It was a lovely event and on the same day a Soapbox Derby was held on St Julians Avenue which was fun for many.

The Guided walks continue, and the Town Carnival is in full swing during July with a week of local bands followed by a week of visiting musicians. In 2017 this included a steel band and a group called El Destino who as I passed one day were belting out songs from Les Miserable. It was a wonderful atmosphere.

On many days, when the cruise ships come to visit, the numerous different accents in and around town are amazing. I work in Market Square and when the cruise ships are in a number of stalls are set up for the visitors to browse and the whole atmosphere can be magical. But if you are planning on driving to town on a cruise day, parking can be restricted so give yourself plenty of time or catch a bus like I do.

The Rocquaine Regatta also takes place in July. The weather wasn't kind for this event in 2017 but a lot of fun was still had down at Rocquaine Bay and of course there was always the beer tent.

At the end of July, or the beginning of August, the annual Scarecrow walk is held in Torteval starting in the fields adjacent to Torteval Church. As you pass through the sign posted route you will see many scarecrow tableaus on display portraying historical figures both international and local to the Island, often in humourous settings.

As part of the walk you will be given the chance to vote for your favourites. There is also a beer tent and food available as well as a number of small stalls offering souvenirs, plants, bric-a-brac and tombolas.

August

In August 2017, we enjoyed the Taste of Guernsey Seafront Sunday on the first Sunday of the month and took home lots of locally produced food for lunch and supper. There is some film of the event on the Visit Guernsey website on:

https://www.facebook.com/VisitGuernsey/videos/101546181 47082312/

During August, Alderney celebrates Alderney Week with a packed events diary which includes a Cavalcade, Rock the Rock, a Festival of Music and fun in the Northern Isle and loads of other events.

This month in 2017 a new State of the Art Driving Range and Crazy Golf course was opened at the St Pierre Park Golf Course. The Crazy Golf is called Pirate Bay Adventure Golf and has a Pirate theme as you can probably guess. Looks like excellent fun and I am hoping to have a go real soon.

August is best known in Guernsey for the shows, starting with the South Show centred around the Sr Martins Community centre, then the West Show out at L'Eree and then finally the North Show at Saumarez Park, which includes the Guernsey Battle of Flowers and all the fun of the fair.

The Donkey Derby also takes place at Saumarez Park in August which is another fun event.

If you are in the Island during this month you should try and get to one of these shows to get a flavor of Guernsey life. For me, West is Best as the phrase goes and that is the show I like to visit. The South is by far the smallest with the North probably claiming the biggest attendance, thanks mainly to the Battle of Flowers.

During August, there are Saturday concerts in the Market Square in the heart of St Peter Port, Sunday concerts at Candie Museum and of course the Guided walks and a range of other events are also taking place while the summer weather holds.

The Harbour Carnival also takes place in August and involves, Duck racing, plastic ducks of course, and the Man Powered Flight Competition.

At the end of the month the Vale Earth Fair stages an open-air music festival at the Vale Castle and there is a Balcony Gig at the Cobo Bay hotel as part of the Bank Holiday weekend.

Pirate Bay Adventure Golf at St Pierre Park

September

The big Guernsey Market takes place in Guernsey during September. The two epic days of food and drink started on the 16th of the month in 2017 with the Live Food Festival.

The Guernsey Food Festival follows on through the month

The annual Battle of Britain air display also takes place in September but sadly on the 14th September 2017 the Red Arrows did not take part. Hopefully they will be back for future years.

There were Proms on the pier on the 9th and Cocktail Week seems to go on forever. There was an Apples, Grapes and Grain Festival in Market Square from the 22nd to the 24th of the month.

In fact, despite the schools going back there are loads of events taking place during the month. The walks continue with the Autumn Walks Festival which includes a huge variety of walks in a number of locations and includes walks in and about Herm. The Saturday Concerts in St Peter Port and the Sunday Concerts in Candie Gardens both continue through the month.

The Sark Roots Festival also takes place in September as do other events in that Island.

October

The Autumn walking festival continues during October but inevitably as the weather takes a turn for the worse and the evenings draw in the number of events start to decline and many of those that continue go indoors.

The Tennerfest starts in October and goes through to mid-November. This is where dozens of local restaurants and hotels across the Islands a range of fixed menus for anything from £10 to £20.

This is a popular event and brings people out to the eateries in their thousands during what could be a quiet time for all the venues.

It is impossible to list all the events that take place so keep an eye of the Visit Guernsey website for the most up to date details where you can search for events at different times of the year and also see what is on during the week of your visit.

The website is www.visitguernsey.com/explore-our-events

November and December

As Tennerfest comes to an end, the Christmas season starts to kick in with businesses organising their Christmas events and the shops setting out their Christmas produce.

St Peter Port and St Sampsons are both decorated with Christmas Trees and lights for the festive occasion and early in December Father Christmas usually visits and turns on the lights.

Market Square Tree

There are many Christmas Fairs organized by local charities where arts and crafts as well as artisan bakers get the chance to sell their wares.

Fresh Fridays continue in Market Square until the end of November and in 2017 there was a Masquerade Ball in aid of the Guernsey Society for the Prevention of Cruelty to Animals.

There are Winter Fayre's at Castle Cornet and late-night shopping sessions take place on Thursday nights in St Peter Port and Tuesday nights on the Bridge.

In 2017 the Friquet Garden Centre set up an excellent Ice Rink which proved very popular and we enjoyed a visit to the Alpine Lodge, set up by the OGH Hotel, complete with selfie ski lift and snow drifting down outside the 'window'.

The mulled cider was excellent, and the schnapps went down a treat as well as the food which included an excellent apple strudel.

The Petit Train ran in 2017 taking people on tours around town to see the Christmas lights and many houses go that extra mile to celebrate the festive season by entering a Christmas lights competition to raise money for charity.

The Herm trident also ran shopping trips to Herm at the weekends for just £1 a head. We were lucky enough to win a trip to Jersey on the Fishing boat "Out the Blue" which was running weekend daytrips to Jersey on the Saturdays before Christmas. That was a real treat.

We also enjoyed a n overnight stay at the Grande Mare on a Quidsin deal which was excellent.

The year ends with a firework display at Castle Cornet and festive parties are held in St Peter Port to see the year out.

General

I haven't listed all the various walking, cycling, coasteering and kayaking tours that run throughout the summer. Again, the tourism website or a visit to the Guernsey Information Centre when you are on the Island will give you all the details

Apart from events there are many Museums and Art Galleries to visit for those interested in the history and culture of the Island.

The Guernsey Museum at Candie Gardens is the largest of the Museums. Castle Cornet has its own displays and a guided walk of the Castle is as entertaining as it is informative.

Fort Grey on the Island's West Coast is also worth a visit as it contains displays concerning the many shipwrecks that have occurred around the Island's coast.

In fact, if you have an interest in Museums you can buy a special ticket which will give you access to all the Government run museums during your stay.

The Guernsey Information Centre

If you like stately homes the nearest equivalent, we have in Guernsey, is Sausmarez Manor. The house is well worth a visit and tours are available, including ghost tours of the House.

In the grounds is a wonderful sculpture park, as well as a model railway and tea garden. If you stop for tea do not miss out on Guernsey Gache, a local fruit loaf, with Guernsey butter.

There is also a regular Farmers Market in the grounds on a Saturday morning during the Spring, Summer and Autumn which is very popular.

During the Occupation of Guernsey in the Second World War, the Germans left many buildings and fortifications, some of which can be accessed during certain times of the week/year.

Memories of those years are still fresh in the minds of many of the older local generation and occasionally you might find someone who will tell you what it was like to live under German rule.

Several museums containing equipment and memorabilia from the occupation have been established, a few in bunkers and facilities left by the Germans. You can find out more on the Festung Guernsey website at:
www.festungguernsey.supanet.com/

If you are interested in the environment you could visit the Ramsar site, a site of special scientific importance at L'Eree and see the wonderful natural flora and fauna that is prolific in this area.

There are many other sites looked after by La Societe Guernesiaise (Tel 01481 725093) including Bird Hides and Orchid fields. You can visit their web site at www.societe.org.gg

For the more adventurous, you could try a Rib Boat Voyage around the coast, including a look at the other Islands and local wildlife such as puffins and perhaps seals and dolphins if you are lucky.

You can also take a tour of the Sark Coast and Caves as we did last summer and enjoy a sing song in these amazing acoustic chambers – see below.

Inside the Sark Caves with Island Rib Voyages

To book your place on one of these unforgettable trips visit:-

http://www.islandribvoyages.com/

Bumblebee Coastal Cruises is another great experience. They can organise cruises, parties and in 2017 ran a regular summer service to Alderney. It is unsure if that will be repeated in 2018. You can find out more at www.bumblebee.gg

Enjoying the power of Bumblebee

If Bumblebee is still running you can enjoy a Skipper experience and get to see for yourself what it is like to Skipper such a great vessel.

For the sporty you have a choice of activities, such as Go Karting, Bowls, Golf, Fishing, Tennis, Table Tennis, Badminton, Coaststeering and Kayaking.

Many other sports are available at the Beau Sejour Leisure Centre. The facilities there include swimming (25 metre, 6 lane pool), table tennis, badminton, tennis, squash and much, much more. They have also recently reopened their Cinema, called Beau Cinema. To see the latest films on show visit https://www.facebook.com/beaucinema/

For the golfers there are three golf courses. Two of them are 18-hole courses, one is linked to the Grande Mare Hotel and the other is at L'Ancresse Common. If you have a handicap you can pay a green fee and play at both courses provided there are no competitions being run on that day.

The nine-hole course is linked to the St Pierre Park Hotel and consists of 9 par threes. There is an excellent driving range attached to the course and a state of the art teaching facility, new for 2017, ideal if you want to practice while on holiday. If you like crazy golf there is an excellent course attached to the St Pierre Park facility and another refurbished crazy golf course at Oatlands which is currently undergoing more developments for 2018.

There are many excellent fishing marks around the Island coast if you would like to try a bit of sea fishing while you are on Guernsey. You can also go on organised fishing trips from the harbour of St Peter Port during the summer. Check out http://www.boatfishing.net/

There is also a surf school based at Vazon and organisations that provide outdoor adventure activities like kayaking and coaststeering such as Outdoor Guernsey, see their website at www.outdoorguernsey.co.uk .

In recent years I have seen people learning to paddle board in Pembroke Bay in the north of the Island and also kite surfing. The seas can be cold though so unless you are a hardened swimmer it might be worth bringing a wetsuit if you plan on learning to surf or paddle board, though hiring kit might be an option.

Many teams come to the Island for sports and at various times of the year sporting festivals are held. Excellent facilities exist for sports like Cricket, Football, Hockey, Rugby, Tennis and Table tennis.

For fishermen there is an International Bass Fishing festival which is held usually every year in August.

A trip to the small Island of Herm is also a must during the summer – take the sun cream though as the sun in Herm seems stronger than in Guernsey, probably due to the clear air, and that's no joke.

In the evenings you can enjoy the Captain's Table at the White House which includes the trip across to Herm, about three miles from St Peter Port Harbour, and a wonderful meal in the hotel with a view back towards Guernsey, framed by the setting sun.

St Peter Port plays host to many clubs and bars for those who like a night out and you can also enjoy the latest movies at our small multi-screen cinema at the Mallard Hotel, which is located near the airport or the Beau Cinema on the outskirts of town.

Places like the Doghouse and some of the livelier bars regularly host live music and occasionally you can find outdoor entertainment, such as summer live music events and balcony concerts at the Cobo Bay Hotel.

Outside theatre is held each year at Castle Cornet, with a season of plays in this brilliant venue, see the Visit Guernsey events diary for details.

Our top 12 days out in Guernsey are as follows:

Day One - Herm

As previously mentioned, a day trip to Herm is a must when visiting Guernsey. The ferries run frequently in the summer months and if you get a really sunny day, the trip will remain in your mind for years to come.

Try and get a seat on the upper deck, so you can take in the marine traffic around St Peter Port, the views of the Islands all around you and of course the sun and sea air. The same location on the return visit will give you exceptional views of Guernsey, St Peter Port and Castle Cornet.

Don't forget the sun cream and your camera. You can enjoy a meal while on the Island and you can shop for beach essentials in the small shops next to the harbour.

For something extra special you can enjoy a stay in the White House Hotel or hire self-catering accommodation. There is also a campsite which is very popular with the Guernsey locals. You can find our more on www.herm.com

Shell Beach - Herm

Day Two - The Little Chapel

This is reputed to be one of the smallest Chapels in the world. Decorated with shells and broken pottery this Chapel was the life's work of one Monk who lived in the adjoining former monastery, now the home of Blanchelande school.

In recent years the students kept the Little Chapel maintained but in 2017 a major refurbishment took place A notice board next to the bus stop by the Chapel explains the history of the building.

While you are visiting, don't forget to pop into Guernsey Clockmakers at the end of the short road where the Chapel is located. Well worth a visit.

Little Chapel, Guernsey

Once you have completed your visit you could make the short journey to visit Bruce Russell, Gold and Silversmith at Le Gron near the airport. They also have the excellent "Mint" restaurant within the grounds.

Entrance to the Farmhouse Hotel

If you prefer somewhere different you are also close to the Farmhouse Hotel where you can enjoy an excellent bar lunch or evening meal.

Day Three – A Sea Adventure around the coast.

Starting from St Peter Port, you can take an Island Rib voyage to the other Islands or along the base of the Island's South Coast Cliffs in one of their fast ribs. It is a stunning adventure and something you will never forget. The tours operate from Easter until October Half term. Full details can be found about these tours on their website at: www.islandribvoyages.com

Photo Courtesy of Island Rib Voyages

BumbleBee is another tour operator that offers tours on the water and trips around the other Islands. Their full name is BumbleBee Coastal Tours and you can see what they offer on their website at www.bumblebee.gg

It is not sure whether or not they will be running in 2018.

Photo Courtesy of Bumblee Tours

They offer several types of tours, private charters and even trips to Alderney in the summer, if the contract is renewed.

If you like fishing you can book a place on a local fishing boat and enjoy some "on the water" experience while hopefully catching some fish. Check out www.boatfishing.net

Day Four - Cliff Walking

The Coastal Cliff paths on Guernsey run from St Peter Port all the way to Pleinmont on the Islands South west corner. If you walked every path you would walk almost 30 miles, as the paths zig zag and double back on themselves in many places. The direct run from St Peter Port to Pleinmont would see you cross a tarmac road in just a couple of places.

The views are generally amazing with a few exceptional vantage points giving you "never to forget" photographic opportunities. Walking the entire length is a daunting prospect and is not recommended but there are three walks we really love to do.

For walk number one you park your car at Corbiere and walk to Le Gouffre for lunch, walking back to help burn off those calories. There are some quite steep elements in this walk so is not for people who have walking difficulties.

My personal favourite is walk number two from the bathing pools in St Peter Port to Fermain Bay for a meal or just an ice-cream, this walk has wonderful views towards the other islands. Park your car by the bathing pools or follow the signs to the Aquarium and you will find the start of the cliff walk.

The Cliffs above Fermain Bay

A sharp set of steps takes you up to the cliff tops and then you follow the path along to Fermain Bay where you drop down to beach level. This walk will take you through the Bluebell woods, an extra bonus in the spring.

Finally, option three is drive to Pleinmont Point and take a walk past the German Fortifications – see below - down to the Imperial Hotel for a meal or a pint, remember it will be all uphill on the way back.

The cliffs can be muddy following wet weather so good walking boots or shoes are a must in those conditions. All have steep sections so if you are not a good walker stick to the upper paths and avoid the steeper sections.

Pleinmont restored Gun Battery

Day Five - Le Guet

Situated on the highest point along the Island's West Coast, the watch house at Le Guet overlooks the stunning bay at Cobo. In this part of Guernsey, the rocks of the coast turn to a golden brown as opposed to the usual grey.

This, along with the often turquoise sea and sandy bay, make the view from this vantage point worth the journey.

The small fort is fascinating in itself having been used by various defenders for many centuries. The pine forest which surrounds the fortification is also quite unique in Guernsey and despite appearances is a recent addition to the area.

Old prints of this area show the watch house standing out above the surrounding area. In the 2nd World War the German Occupiers built fortifications into the hill which must have had uninterrupted views of the horizon.

If you visit during the evening, watch out for the ghostly figure of a German soldier patrolling the viewing area still looking out to sea for signs of an invasion or a passing ship.

Le Guet from Cobo Bay

Day Six - The Occupation Museums

Since the 2nd World War, several museums containing artifacts from the Occupation, have sprung up, some in the actual fortifications themselves.

Probably the oldest of these is the Guernsey Occupation museum near the Airport. This provides an interesting insight into life during the Occupation.

Others include a museum at Havelet Bay, which occupies the site of some massive fuel tanks which were hidden in the hillside. These were probably used to fuel U-Boats. The German Underground Hospital doesn't have many exhibits but is a powerful demonstration of German life underground and how they used slave labour to create these huge structures.

On certain dates you can also visit a restored bunker at Vazon to see how the troops lived and if you are fit, you can climb to the top of one of the watch towers at Pleinmont. This climb however is by runged ladders and not for anyone who isn't physically fit and able to climb a ladder.

The Pleinmont headland is particularly well fortified and there you can see a recently excavated trench-work and coastal battery, with a large gun in place. Again at certain times of the year, enactments are held and the gun is fired.

Another must visit is the German Naval HQ next to the Collenette Hotel in St Peter Port. This bunker has been partly restored and features a film show which includes interviews with one of the German officers who worked in the bunker during the war.

It is a fascinating insight into the life of the troops who occupied the Island and shows how the bunker was utilized during the war years.

Underground Hospital

Day Seven - L'Eree / Lihou Island.

The land around the Lihou Island Headland has been designated a Ramsar site. The area includes the large shingle bank which protects the low-lying wetland which is known locally as the L'Eree Aerodrome.

This was actually where planes landed before the current airport was built prior to the 2nd World War.

The area of beach in front of the shingle bank is also protected and is a popular spot for bird watchers.

Nature Reserve at L'Eree

A good viewing point is near the entrance to the large dolmen in the area, near the tower in the above photograph.

If you can find the small rough car park on the hill next to the dolmen and in the shadow of the large German watchtower you can then walk around to the entrance and take in the view. The Dolmen is what is known as a passage grave and is called locally Le Creux es Faies, when you pop in to look around don't forget to look out for the fairies!

If you walk or drive down to the L'Eree Headland Car Park you will be able to look across to Lihou Island. This small Island is connected to Guernsey at low tide by a causeway but when the tide comes in it is cut off. If you are planning a visit to Lihou be aware of the tides. A notice board by the start of the causeway should give you up to date tidal information.

You should be aware that there are no toilet facilities on the Island and the lone house is only used for part of the year.

One last thing to look at in this area is the memorial to the poor souls that died on the MV Prosperity when she ran aground on a reef near Lihou Island on the 16th January 1974.

It is a reminder of the many vessels and the hundreds of lives that have been lost in the treacherous seas around these Islands.

Day Eight - Castle Cornet and other Guernsey Museums

Castle Cornet has guarded the entrance to St Peter Port for over 800 years and is the flagship attraction of the Guernsey Museums service. In recent years they have offered a special entrance ticket which will allow you to get in to the Castle, the Candie Museum and Fort Grey during your stay on the Island. If museums are on your "must do" list while you are on Guernsey this is a must buy ticket.

Castle Cornet, St Peter Port, Guernsey

During the summer, many re-enactments are carried out in the Castle and in some of the other historical locations like Fort Grey. This living history tells the story of Guernsey in an easy to understand and fun way.

The Guernsey Information Centre will have details of what is going on during your stay as will the events page on the Visit Guernsey website.

Other places to visit include the Martello Tower at Rousse which has a fortified defence, including replica cannons.

An explanation of how the Islands Martello Towers were networked around the North of the Island to provide an overlapping defensive system are also in a display housed in the small stone building below the Martello Tower.

Each Martello tower had a similar building and these housed the gunpowder and munitions for each tower.

Entry is free during the summer season but the tower may be locked in the winter.

Many of the Islands defences have explanatory boards which describe the origins of the defences and how they formed part of the Islands overall defensive strategy.

Martello Tower at L'Ancresse.

Day Nine - A Walking Tour of St Peter Port

Particularly during the summer there are many organised walking tours of St Peter Port. These are carried out by accredited guides and take in the long and often colourful history of this amazing town.

One we had great fun on was an evening Ghost walk through the back streets of the town. This was conducted by Annette Henry who specialises in Guernsey folklore tours. This culminated with a nice meal in one of the town's fine restaurants, to help us warm up from the chill of the night and the chill of the many "haunting" stories.

Details of the various walks on offer and the starting times and meeting points can be found in the Guernsey Information Centre.

More information about Annette Henry and the various tours she can offer can be found on her website at: https://annettehenrytours.gg/

St Peter Port, Guernsey.

Day Ten - Go Karting family fun Day Out

Track Lane, near the boundary between the parishes of St Peter Port and St Sampsons, on the Island's east coast has long been a popular sporting venue on Guernsey. Home, until recent years, of the Island's premier football stadium, it also hosts a go karting track which runs around the perimeter of the pitch.

Many go karting events are held here during the year but when official races aren't being held you can hire a kart and have a go yourself. This is a popular way for families to compete against each other and as a way for many to get their first experience of single seat motor racing.

Alongside "The Track" was the MFA Guernsey Bowl. Unfortunately, this closed down in 2017 and there is no indication that the facility will open again.

You can find out more about Go-Karting in Guernsey at:

www.kartingguernsey.co.uk

If you want to visit another attraction before or after your go-karting experience, a trip to Oatlands, a short drive away, is worth a visit. You can eat there and currently more attractions are being developed as I type. There is a crazy golf course and several things for young children to do as well as a range of shops and of course the original brick kilns.

There are dozens of alternatives if you like different types of sport, many of which are mentioned in this Handbook.

The Brick Kilns at Oatlands

Day Eleven - Victor Hugo's House Tour

Open from April to September, Victor Hugo's House in Guernsey is well worth a visit. Victor Hugo is arguably Guernsey's most famous resident of all time. He spent most of his 19 years in exile from France in Guernsey and wrote most of his famous book Les Miserables while living in his home in St Peter Port.

To get a flavour of what you can see in this amazing house have a look at their website at www.victorhugo.gg

Tours of the house are held at certain times of the day so please contact the house or the Guernsey Information Centre before planning your visit.

You are unlikely to get a space on a tour if you just pitch up but you can normally get access to the gardens at the rear of the house.

Day Twelve - Trip to Sark

Last, but certainly by no means least, is a visit to the fourth largest of the Channel Islands. Sark has its own website (www.sark.info) which explains all about the Island, how to get there and what to do while you are there.

There are no cars on Sark, which means to get around you will need to either walk, bicycle, take a tractor ride or enjoy a horse drawn carriage tour of the Island.

Welcome message on the tunnel at Maseline Harbour, Sark

There is much to see, some delightful hotels if you fancy a longer stay and some good food to be enjoyed.

Sark has such an interesting story to tell, worth a book of its own, especially the story of the occupation of the Island during the Second World War. As a place to visit, it is great if you like beautiful views, peace and tranquility. It is also listed as a special dark skies location for the budding astronomers amongst you.

If you are looking for something more active then it may not be for you, unless you like sheep racing! (see the Sark Events Diary)

There is more on how to get to Sark later in the book.

Eating Out

Guernsey is blessed with many wonderful restaurants offering a range of different cuisines including English, French, Italian, Indian, Thai and Chinese; plus many more.

If you want a take-away there are several options for Pizzas, Chinese, Indian and English food. You can also enjoy a fish and chip meal from several excellent chippies around the Island. Beetons and the Cobo Fish and Chip shop being at the top of our list.

Several restaurants have excellent reputations and are well supported by the locals – always a good sign.

To help you enjoy the most of your time we have listed our favourite restaurants below. The list is in no particular order but during this last year we have seen a few new restaurants join the list, the Slaughterhouse and Nineteen Bar and Grill foremost amongst them.

Al Fresco on the Terrace at Moore's Hotel

You should note that smoking is banned in all enclosed public spaces, such as Restaurants, Bars and Clubs.

This means you should enjoy your meal without worrying about smoke. However, if you like a smoke with your meal you may find a few places where you can enjoy a meal outside, weather permitting.

A list of our favourite eating places with telephone numbers is included in the appendix at the end of the book. It looks like we eat out a lot!!

The last on this list is part of a group of restaurants which we like to frequent as they have an excellent loyalty scheme called the Inndulgence Club. To see the full list of their restaurants in Guernsey and Jersey and their current menus have a look at www.liberationgroup.com

Don't forget in the summer during most of the seafront Sundays, when the main road in closed, many of the restaurants on the seafront go 'al fresco' and set up their tables in the road outside their premises. These are enjoyed by locals and visitors alike and even the cruise passengers sometimes stop and enjoy an impromptu lunch in the sunshine and watch the world go by.

Indian Meal Al Fresco on a Seafront Sunday

Shopping

For most people a visit to the shops and the buying of souvenirs are essential parts of a holiday. St Peter Port, the Island's capital, is where you will find the majority of the shops.

The High Street and the Commercial Arcade form the core shopping area with extensions of the main shopping area going to the North down the Pollet and to the South up the Bordage, around the restored Market Buildings and on to the old quarter, which is home to a range of small quirky shops. It is antique hunter heaven.

Some well-known names can be found in town, as it is known, such as M&S, Miss Selfridge, Next, Boots, Mountain Warehouse, Schu and Fatface. Amongst these are local shops selling a wide range of goods including perfumes, jewellery, technology goods, souvenirs and clothing. There is no VAT in Guernsey, so prices should be competitive.

Town is the serious place to shop but out of town there are many hidden treasures for the serious shopper.

The Bridge as it known is the second largest shopping centre on the Island with a range of small shops serving the populous areas around St Sampsons and the Vale.

In recent years it has become a popular place for Charity shops but in amongst them are some excellent jewellery and clothing outlets which includes the Diamond Museum at Ray and Scott, one of the Island's top jewellers.

Out of these built up areas you can find possibly the Island's top jewellery outlet near the Airport. Bruce Russell is a world-renowned Goldsmith and his premises, which includes a restaurant and beautiful gardens, is definitely worth a visit.

St Martins has a small shopping center with food and gift shops as well as local clothing and furniture stores and is also worth a visit.

The Island also boasts some impressive garden centres and amongst these Le Friquet Garden Centre stands out. It has a wide range of products above the usual plants and gardening paraphernalia, including clothes and household items. It also has a very nice tea room and restaurant.

At Christmas in 2017 it housed an Ice Rink and had a spectacular grotto area, including singing reindeers.

All shops accept English currency, and a few will accept Euros. The normal credit cards are usually accepted in all but the charity shops.

There are plenty of cash points in town and on the bridge.

Getting Around

Whether you arrive by sea or air, you will need to get around the Island, starting with the trip to your hotel. Bearing in mind that the Island is only 24 square miles in size, nowhere is going to be very far away.

Taxis are usually waiting for you at the Airport and at the Harbour though at peak times you may have to wait. You can avoid the wait by booking a taxi before you arrive. The driver will show you to your hotel, and if you engage him in conversation may even tell you what's happening while you are on the Island.

Buses are also available from the Airport if you are just seeking a run into St Peter Port. If you fancy exploring by bus we recommend you get yourself a bus timetable or download their app' as soon as you arrive and plan your days. The coastal run can be fun and at certain times of the day will take you all the way around the Island.

However, the buses do not run late at night so if you are planning a bus trip and an evening meal, check out the timetable to be sure you can get back. All trips cost a flat rate of £1.00 (2017 rates). If you are planning to use the bus often during your stay you can buy a Puffin Pass which reduces your journey costs to 55p. This can reduce the cost of travel considerably.

For a complete Guide to the local bus services please visit their website at www.buses.gg.

On that website, you can download the bus timetable by clicking on the Bus Services link.

Bicycles can be hired if you are feeling fit and want to explore on two wheels. Electric bikes are also available which will take away some of the strain. However, the Island's roads are narrow so be careful if you are not totally confident on a bike. Cars and larger vehicles can get very close to you and there are precious few cycle tracks. It is also illegal to cycle on the pavements.

Scooters and motorbikes can be hired and can be a fun option but be careful on the narrow roads.

For many who come by sea, bringing the car with all the things you want and the capacity to take back all those souvenirs is a great option. It is vitally important that as soon as you get off the boat you are aware of the differences between driving in Guernsey and elsewhere.

As with the UK, we drive on the left. The maximum speed limit is 35mph and in some built up areas, coastal areas and around schools, this can be reduced to 25mph or 20mph. Diversions, due to road works, are frequent so a good road map to help you find your way around is vital.

Road names are mostly in French, if you can find them, and directional signs tend to be pretty general in content and few and far between, though many of the main tourist attractions are quite well sign posted with the standard international brown signs.

There are a few roundabouts, but many locals are not very good with these, so be careful. However, the biggest factor to be aware of is the widely used "Filter in Turn" system.

These are signposted with an inverted triangle, stating "Filter in Turn" in advance of the junction, while the junction itself has a yellow hatch, box junction painted on the road. The words Filter in Turn are also usually painted on the road on the approach to the junction.

The idea of these junctions is that traffic takes it in turns to cross, as it says on the sign, you filter in turn. It is important to watch out for these junctions, particularly where traffic is faster moving, as a car coming from a side road on to the filter will have priority if they reach the junction before you.

When travelling around you will see yellow arrows in the road. This isn't a one-way system, as many believe. These arrows warn you that a yellow line, a stop junction, is coming up – usually 25 yards away. Yellow lines along the side of the road mean no parking at any time; we don't have double yellow lines in the Island.

Parking is also different. Currently there is no charge for parking though changing to paid parking is always being considered. Currently there are no plans to introduce paid parking that I am aware of.

In St Peter Port and in many public car parks around the island you will need to set a clock and be aware of the amount of time you can stay in the various disc zones.

By and large the closer to the town centre, the less time you will have to park. Generally, the zones run for ½ hour, 1 hour, 2 hours, 3 hours, 5 hours and 10 hours. Large blue signs will tell you what is permitted.

Long term parking is at a premium in St Peter Port so if you are planning a trip to Herm for the day, be careful where you park, or perhaps get a bus or taxi into town for the day.

Parking clocks can be bought from the Guernsey Information Centre, the local Police Station in town or from many stores and garages around the Island. They cost a few pounds. Failure to set a clock properly, or overstaying the amount of time permitted in the parking zone, can result in a fine.

Obviously, all of the above applies to drivers whether they bring their own car or hire a car while on the Island. Hire cars are relatively cheap so for a short stay they can be the more cost effective. You should be given a parking clock and road advice when you collect the vehicle.

It is also worth noting that the price of petrol has risen quite a lot in recent years and is roughly the same as in the UK, maybe even more these days. A full tank is more than likely to last you a couple of weeks unless you decide to drive around the Island until you get giddy!!

The Other Islands

Guernsey is blessed to be part of a group of Islands, all within easy reach of each other and all with their own unique character. In order of proximity to Guernsey we will run through those that are accessible, all year round.

Lihou Island

Accessible on foot at low tide, Lihou Island is located off the Island's West Coast near L'Eree Bay. It has a ruined priory which has been the subject of extensive archaeological work over many years. There is a single building on the Island which is used as a Youth Hostel from time to time.

There is a warning about the tides at the start of the causeway and we recommend you read this carefully. On certain days you can walk across in the morning, enjoy being cut off during the day and having the Island almost to yourself and then walk back in the evening.

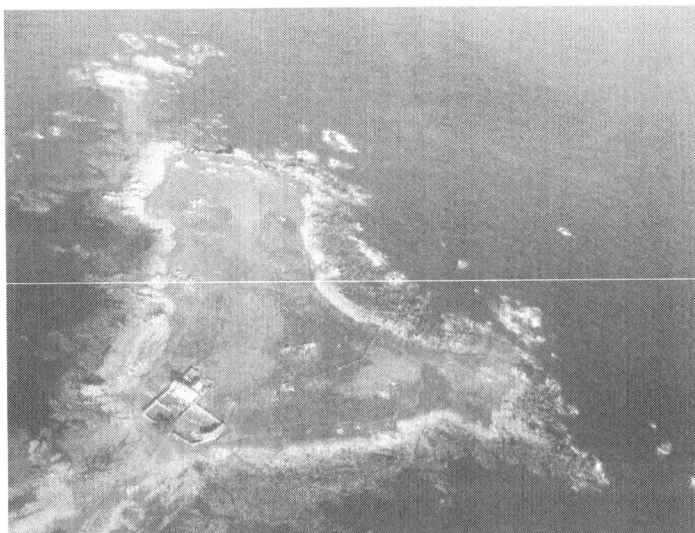

Lihou Island from the air

However, there are no toilet facilities on the Island, shops for refreshments or telephones.

A recent story of interest was the discovery of a range of unexploded shells on the Island. Apparently, the Germans used Lihou Island for target practice during the occupation!

Herm

Situated some three miles to the East of Guernsey, Herm is the main playground for the Islands boating fraternity and those that have fallen in love with this beautiful small Island. A short, 30-minute, boat ride from St Peter Port will take you to Herm Harbour or to Rosaire Steps, according to the tide.

The White House Hotel looks out towards Guernsey and is a lovely place to stay if you want to get away from it all. There are no cars on Herm and few roads. The few permanent residents either walk or rely on tractors for transport. There is also a camp site and many Islanders enjoy a week or two there in the summer.

Shell Beach in Herm

The Mermaid is the main bar for the Island and they do excellent bar meals. You can also buy your supplies there if you decide to camp.

Walking across the Island you will soon find yourself at Shell Beach or Belvoir Bay. Both beaches are amazing suntraps. A walk all the way around the Island is worth the effort and will give you great views of the other Islands in the Bailiwick.

For full details check out the Herm website at www.herm.com

Travel Tips and Links:

Trident Ferries offer regular trips to the Island starting at 8am. You will be given a time when you must come back. Don't miss the boat. Adult fares in 2017 were £13 return for adults and £6.50 for children

For up to date information on trips to Herm visit - http://www.traveltrident.com/

Sark

A much longer boat trip away (60 minutes), Sark is a different world and well worth a visit. You can enjoy a day trip to Sark but it is so beautiful you may want to stay a bit longer. It does have several excellent hotels but unfortunately several were closed during 2015 and still hadn't reopened in 2017.

The Town Centre in Sark! (Photo courtesy of J Moore)

Travel from Maseline Harbour to the top of the hill is either by foot or by the toast rack (see below), a tractor drawn trailer. This costs £1.10 for adults and £0.55 for children (2016 rates).

When you arrive, if you are staying in Sark, your bags are automatically taken to your hotel, make sure your bags are labelled. You walk through a tunnel to the waiting toast rack or if you are feeling very fit you can walk up the hill. Not for the faint hearted! Once at the top of the hill, you can hire a bike or a horse drawn carriage and explore this Island of tranquility.

The tunnel to Maseline Harbour in Sark.

The Island has a few shops and a good bar or two, if you feel the need to take a break and enjoy a drink.

The Seigneurie Gardens are worth a visit and while looking around the Island you will discover the strange laws that still rule this unique Island.

The way taxes are paid and land is owned is feudal in origin and the Seigneur has unique powers. Cars are forbidden on the Island, as is flying over the Island – the exception being visits by royalty.

Take a torch for walking around in the evenings as they have no street lighting.

As a result of those dark nights, Sark has special dark sky status making it a wonderful place for anyone interested in astronomy.

The view down from La Coupee.
(Photo courtesy of J Moore)

From Sark you can see Jersey clearly as well as the coast of France.

In 2016 we had the pleasure of visiting Sark for my son's wedding. We stayed at the wonderful Stock's Hotel which was excellent with great food and friendly staff. I would highly recommend this Hotel to anyone looking for a bit of luxury when visiting Sark. We also ate at Hathaway's in the Seigneurie Gardens and the food there was wonderful.

We took a Horse drawn carriage to the ceremony and that was an experience not to be missed, especially if, like me, you had never been in a horse drawn vehicle before.

Some of the roads are pretty basic so good walking shoes are essential. The "short cut" path down to Stocks Hotel was literally just a path alongside fields of sheep so we were pleased the weather was dry, especially when we came back from the wedding in our "finery".

There is a Gold Bollard at the harbor, marking the achievement of Sark born John Guille in becoming a powerboat world champion in the UIM Class 3A World Offshore Powerboat Championships which were held in Guernsey in 2014. Also look out for the Gold Letter Box, which celebrates the gold medal that Sark born Carl Hester won in the 2012 Olympics.

For more information on Sark visit www.sark.info
Travel Tips and Links:

The Isle of Sark Shipping Company offers regular sailings to Sark. www.sarkshippingcompany.com

As regards finding somewhere to stay, with the current uncertainty about the opening of several of the hotels in 2018, we suggest you visit:

www.sark.co.uk/where-to-stay/

Alderney

Travelling to Alderney is usually by plane but in 2017, Bumblebee Coastal Cruises offered sailings to Alderney in the summer. However it is unclear if that will happen again in 2018.

Aurigny fly there on a regular basis and landing there is a unique experience, particularly if you are only used to travelling in bigger planes.

Braye Beach, Alderney

The Island is the third largest of the Channel Islands and the most northerly. It has an amazing breakwater, which was built by the British to provide a safe anchorage for the British fleet.

For the ultimate in luxury stays, book a night at the Braye Beach Hotel. The photo above was taken from that hotel - www.brayebeach.com

Alderney has many good hotels and guest houses, a 9-hole golf course and some great pubs. It has blonde hedgehogs and just off the coast there is an amazing Gannet Colony at Les Etac. In fact, standing on the cliffs, watching and listening to the sounds of the colony is an amazing experience.

The Gannet Colony off Alderney

The tides around Alderney can be extremely fast and I have watched a boat moving backwards against the stream, so if you are sailing over yourself, take special note of the tides. You may save yourself a lot of time.

In the Second World War, the Alderney population was evacuated and the Island was used as a concentration camp by the Germans.

The population wasn't allowed back until the 15th December 1945, well after the war was over.

That day is celebrated annually as Home Coming Day.

A sombre war memorial to the slave labourers who died during the occupation is a poignant reminder of those awful days.

The War Memorial in Alderney

Alderney must be one of the most heavily defended locations in the world with forts dotted around everywhere. It is now the place to be for on-line gambling companies with many of the big names holding licences to operate from the island. It is arguably the only true Channel Island with all the others being located in the Bay of St Malo.

Alderney week during August is their big festival but book your accommodation and travel early as the Island is very busy that week.

The Braye Beach Hotel ,Alderney

Travel Tips and Links:

Air travel to Alderney is available allyear round by Aurigny in one of their Dorniers. To make a booking visit www.aurigny.com

BumbleBee may offer trips to Alderney in season. For more information visit their website at www.bumblebee.gg

Our favourite hotel in Alderney is the Braye Beach Hotel – see photo. www.brayebeach.com

Jersey

If you are visiting Guernsey and have time to spare, a quick flight to the biggest of the Channel Islands is worth taking.

The West Coast of Jersey from La Moye

The flight time by Flybe is about 10 minutes. Waves, the new Air Taxi service, started operating in the autumn of 2017 and they offer inter-island flights too for a fixed price of £65 each way (as of December 2017).

If you do fly to Jersey, a great way to get to the town is to jump on the Number 15 bus to St Helier, which runs every 20 minutes from the airport terminal. It costs just £2 per person. They operate double decker buses on this route, so you can get a splendid view of Jersey's south coast on your way into town. St Helier, the capital of Jersey, is more commercial than St Peter Port in Guernsey and the waterfront is getting quite built up but it has a vibrancy all of it's own and the town has a great range of shops to choose from.

Unlike Guernsey, they still have their traditional market, which is well worth a visit. On our last trip in December 2017 we had a great lunch in Hugo's which is right opposite one of the main entrances to the Market. We also enjoyed a lovely hot chocolate in the market itself on one rainy day.

Jersey Market

From St Helier you can get a bus to almost anywhere on the Island from the bus terminus which is hidden right in the sea front area of town, close to the Pomme D'Or Hotel. Most people during a visit will head to the impressive Jersey Zoo but there are many other attractions including the excellent Lavender Farm and of course Jersey Pottery.

The zoo was established by the late Gerald Durrell and it specialises in conservation work. You can easily spend a day just looking around this beautiful zoo, taking particular note of the famous Gorillas and of course the Meerkats. In fact, you can find out more and even adopt a Jersey Meerkat at http://www.durrell.org/home/meerkat/

Like Guernsey, Jersey was also occupied during the second world war and to mark their liberation in 1945 a wonderful statue was installed in Liberation Square on the 50th anniversary – see photo.

Jersey Liberation Monument in St Helier

Jersey is also blessed with some fabulous Hotels and Restaurants so while you are there take in a meal in the shadow of Gorey Castle or sit outside at St Aubin and look out towards St Helier and Elizabeth Castle.

For Christmas, the area in front of the Royal Yacht Hotel is converted into a winter wonderland for the annual Feté de Noué. When we visited there was music and entertainment and as we were staying in the Royal Yacht hotel we had the benefit of all the sights and sounds from our room. During our visit in 2017 we were too early for this event but there were many stalls set up in the Royal Square and we enjoyed a lovely Mulled Cider while watching Morris Dancers entertaining the crowds.

If you choose to stay at the Royal Yacht over the festive season and you are a light sleeper and like an early night, it may be better if you choose a room that doesn't look out over the event space. It can get quite lively.

Feté de Noué stalls outside Royal Yacht Hotel

Travel Tips and links:

You can travel to Jersey either by plane using Flybe, see our travel links section. You can also travel to Jersey from Guernsey by boat on Condor.

For more information about Jersey visit www.jersey.com

Our favourite hotel in Jersey is the Royal Yacht which is in St Helier. For a special treat visit just before Christmas and enjoy the Feté de Noué.

www.theroyalyacht.com

And Finally

When you start spending money on the Island you will be amazed to get your change in Guernsey's own currency. The Guernsey pound is equivalent to the UK pound, so you will have no exchange differences to worry about but whereas you can spend British pounds in Guernsey, you can't spend your Guernsey money in the UK.

You can spend Guernsey currency in any of the Channel Islands, but it isn't accepted in the UK.

You will also find £1 notes in your change rather than the £1 coin. The coins are legal tender in the Island but not well used. Many people take a £1 note back as a souvenir.

Guernsey coins are different too so make sure you check your change before you leave and try and change any Guernsey notes for English one's before you go home.

To conclude this book, we have listed below 2 web sites that we hope you will find useful if you want to carry out any further research into Guernsey before making your journey.

Guernsey Government Web Site: www.gov.gg

Visit Guernsey Web Site: www.visitguernsey.com

Useful Numbers:

Guernsey Police
Tel: 01481 725111

Beau Sejour Leisure Centre (Bookings)
Tel: 01481 747200

Princess Elizabeth Hospital (including A & E)
Tel: 01481 725241

As a final word, there is currently no reciprocal medical agreement between Guernsey and the UK which means if you do get ill while on the Island you will need to pay for your medical treatment. Guernsey is a separate jurisdiction and has no National Health Service as there is in the UK. Guernsey people have to pay for visits to the Doctor and Dentist, although there is a scheme which covers locals for any essential major treatment they require.

We hope you enjoyed reading this Handbook and thank you for your purchase. If you find something you feel we have missed or could be changed, please let us know by emailing us at tonybrassell@gmail.com

We look forward to seeing you on Guernsey soon and hope that by sharing our knowledge and experience with you we help make your visit to the Island a great experience.

The Author

This handbook has been compiled and written by Tony Brassell. He was born and raised in the Island and has lived there all his life. He spent a long career in the Civil Service, acquiring a wide knowledge of Guernsey and has a keen interest in the Island's heritage and culture, in a wide range of areas.

He spent many years acting as the Island's native guide, within the Civil Service, and has escorted VIP's at the highest level, including a Deputy Prime Minister, when they have visited Guernsey.

When he left the Civil Service, he established a local tour company called Experience Guernsey Limited and operated that business until 2008. He is now concentrating on his work as a Business Advisor with the Guernsey Enterprise Agency, trading as Startup Guernsey (www.startup.gg) and he is also the Branch Office for the IoD Guernsey Branch.

He builds, hosts and maintains websites for businesses and private individuals through the domain www.bestplace4u.co.uk and is a freelance writer.

He was a single handicap golfer and in 2012 was Captain of the L'Ancresse Golf Club but has now had to retire from the sport due to ill health.

His unique perspective on Guernsey through a lifetime based on the Island, and years of promoting the Island, make him an ideal Author of this Handbook. He promised to give an honest appraisal of Guernsey, explaining what works and what doesn't.

Importantly if you are planning a stay on the Island, he believes that you should make the most of your time, seeing as much as you can, while still taking time to relax and enjoy the peace and quiet that is easily found on this beautiful British Channel Island.

Other books by Tony include **Ten Days One Guernsey Summer**, a story linked to the Evacuation of the Island in June 1940. This is available in local bookshops and on Amazon as a paperback or on Kindle.

Appendices

Hotels

L'Atlantique Hotel	01481 264056
Cobo Bay Hotel	01481 257102
La Grande Mare Hotel	01481 256576
The OGH	01481 724921
Moores Hotel	01481 724452
Duke of Richmond	01481 726221
La Fregate	01481 724624
Havelet Hotel	01481 722199
St Pierre Park	01481 728282
Hougue Du Pommier	01481 256531
The Bella Luce	01481 238764
La Barbarie	01481 235217
Jerbourg Hotel	01481 238826
Les Douvres	01481 238731
Fermain Valley Hotel	01481 235666
Farmhouse Hotel	01481 264181
L'Auberge du Val	01481 263862
Imperial Hotel	01481 264044
La Trelade	01481 235454
La Villette	01481 235292
The Peninsula Hotel	01481 248400
Les Rocquettes	01481 722146
Saints Bay Hotel	01481 238888

Guest Houses

La Roche Guest House	01481 258088
Charmaine Guest House	01481 245583
Anneville Guest House	01481 263814
Castaways Guest House	01481 239010
El Tabora Guest House	01481 721341
Grisnoir Guest House	01481 727267

Self-Catering Apartments

Vazon Bay	01481 254353
Adair Bungalows	01481 253991
La Barbarie Apartments	01481 235217
La Grande Mare	01481 256576
Rocquaine Bay	01481 254353
The Bay, Pembroke	01481 247573
Wisteria	01481 257113
L'Aumone House Barn	01481 256841

Restaurants

The Slaughterhouse	01481 712123
La Fregate Hotel	01481 724624
Pier 17 -	01481 720823
L'Auberge	01481 238485
La Grande Mare	01481 256576
Le Nautique	01481 721714
Mora's	01481 751053
Da Nellos	01481 721552
Cobo Bay Hotel	01481 257102
Hotel de Havelet	01481 722199
La Perla	01481 712127
Petit Bistro	01481 725055
Marina Restaurant	01481 247066
Beach House	01481 246494
Crabby Jacks	01481 257489
Christies	01481 726624
Village East	01481 700100
Urban Kitchen	01481 736366
The Boathouse	01481 700061
Dix Neuf	01481 723455
Deerhound	01481 238585
Fleur du Jardin	01481 257996
Bella Luce	01481 238764
Imperial Hotel	01481 264044
Longfrie Inn	01481 263107
Terrace Tea Garden	01481 724478
Deerhound Inn	01481 238585
Pony Inn	01481 244374
Octopus	01481 722400
19 Bar and Grill	01481 740019
The Dragon Chinese Restaurant	01481 244688
The Indian Cottage	01481 244820
The Kiln	01481 245661
Houmet Tavern	01481 242214

While every effort is made to ensure the content of this handbook is accurate, no responsibility for any loss or damages arising from the contents and use of this book will be accepted. Any suggestions or recommendations made in the book are made in good faith and based on our knowledge and experiences. Things change over time and current standards may not always be as high as when we last visited the various premises.

If you would like to be included in this book, or have any comments or views concerning the content, please contact the author by email at: tony@bestplace4u.co.uk.

32762840R00061

Printed in Great Britain
by Amazon